Horatius Flaccus

The Church Knaviad

Horace in West Haven

Horatius Flaccus

The Church Knaviad
Horace in West Haven

ISBN/EAN: 9783744661454

Printed in Europe, USA, Canada, Australia, Japan

Cover: Foto ©Lupo / pixelio.de

More available books at **www.hansebooks.com**

THE CHURCH KNAVIAD,

OR

HORACE IN WEST HAVEN.

A SLIGHT TOUCH OF THE

SERIO-COMIC,

TOUCHING

CHURCH KNAVERY.

BY HORATIUS FLACCUS.

NEW HAVEN:

PUBLISHED BY DR. FAUSTUS,

No. 89 HIGH-OLD-FLEET-STREET.

1864.

PREFACE.

Prefaces are never read. They never should be. They are like corks to bottles, only intended to retain the flavor of the vintage or keep down the effervescence for the flagon. None but downright nincompoops ever taste of the cork. If you would read this volume, therefore, cut the preface at once, and let the cork fly. If the vintage that follows is not to your liking,—if you do not agree with us that it sparkles with genuine wit, humor, and pathos, then, with Dogberry, write yourself down an ass, and therein your judgment will accord for once with that of

DR. FAUSTUS.

THE CHURCH KNAVIAD,
OR
HORACE IN WEST HAVEN.

CANTO I.

I do not like you, Dr. Pell,
The reason why, I cannot tell;
But this I know, and that full well,
I do not like you, Dr. Pell!
Hudibras.

SCENE IN WEST HAVEN.—*Horace and Mæcenas enter town.—The latter recounts his adventurous escape from the dominions of Pluto—in the vulgate, "Old Scratch;" while the former writes a veritable history, &c., &c., with a slight episode on the town.*

I.
My dear Mæcenas, how d'you do?
Quite unexpected meeting you,
   So far away from home;
I really thought you in arrears
To Pluto still a thousand years,
   For what you did at Rome.

II.
"My sins, you see, the chief amount,
Were posted to the wrong account,
   By Satan's clerk *pro tem.*
So here's my clearance and discharge,
And liberty to roam at large,
   O'er this old ball again."

III.

You were indeed a "lucky chiel,"
To come it o'er the subtle deil
    In such a way as that;
A bribe? ah, yes, the very trick
You played at Tusculum so slick,
    Did Satan smell the rat?

IV.

" No, not exactly; but he looked
To see if each account was booked,
    And paged in order right;
And then he scratched his dexter brow,
And said, he rather guessed 'as how'
    I could'nt come it quite!

V.

" To which I civilly rejoined,
Just as your Majesty's inclined,
    Not as I care a groat;
For since my passport is *visœd*,
And the grim ferryman is paid,
    And stands within his boat,

VI.

" Ready to waft me back again,
With the first breeze from Stygian plain,
    I don't exactly see
How a *ne exeat* will lie,
Unless your Majesty deny
    The right of Charon's fee.

VII.

"At this he stamped his hoof and swore
He'd batter down all h—ll before
    He'd have such emigration;
It was enough to make one swear
Terrific oaths on nether air,
    Or damn a new creation!

VIII.

"His realm, he said, would shortly be
Depopulated, and set free
    From every honest knave,
If Charon were allowed to take
Just whom he pleased across the lake,
    Without his sovereign leave.

IX.

"But heeding not his wrathful mood,
I still more resolutely stood
    By what I'd said before;
And giving Charon, first the wink,
And then his *obolus* or "chink,"
    We darted from the shore.

X.

"And now across the Stygian lake,
And fiercely bellowing in our wake,
    Old Cerebus doth come,
With all his hundred-headed pack
Of barking whelps upon our track,
    To rend the infernal dome.

XI.

"But Charon plies his dusky oar,
And soon the dark Plutonian shore
    Recedes from mortal sight,
With all the wild infernal din
Of shrieking dervishes within
    Its halls of dismal light.

XII.

"And now at length, we stand again
On terra firma's firm domain,
    Untrammelled and set free;
And henceforth bound to see the 'sights,'
The desperate raids and bloody fights,
    In 'Young America.'

XIII.

"For here we find the very air
Sonorous with the din of war,
    And the loud-clashing steel,
With brazen cannon belching forth
The thunders of the indignant North,
    In bomb and shrieking shell:

XIV.

"A sight at which the angels grieve,
And devils chuckle in their sleeve,
    To see the horrid farce,
Of thousands rushing on their doom,
'Mid shot, and shell, and rattling bomb,
    All for a biped race!

XV.

"How little thought we in old Rome,
That such a day as this would come,
    When pure Phœnician blood
Would flow like rivers to give place
To that of Afric's dusky race,
    Beyond Hesperia's flood!

XVI.

"Would that the immortal gods could rise,
And frown indignant from the skies
    Upon this direful scene;
Where brother, seeking brother's blood,
Defiles the land with corpses strewed
    From Mexico to Maine!

XVII.

"No wonder that all hell was bent
On being fiercely jubilant,
    In 'Eighteen-Sixty-three;'
It proves the devil's harvest year,
As wrote the ancient king and seer
    In book of prophesy!

XVIII.

"But see you group of merry faces,
There the genius of the place is,
    Now louder peals the laughter,
By Jove! with them how passing well
The motto—*vive la bagatelle*;
    'Tis Upson they are after!"

XIX.

To this digression had he come,
My patron once in lofty Rome,
    When first we struck the earth;
And taking now our bearings, found
We'd hit the "Rock House on the Sound,"
    A scene of joy and mirth.

XX.

For here our jovial landlord stands,
A "host" among a host of friends,
    As the swift jest goes round;
And swifter dimes accumulate,
From early morn till evening late,
    In merry tinkling sound!

XXI.

He hath a fund of humorous joke
To crack the sides of honest folk,
    And to dispel *ennui*;
And tells them with such *naivete*,
And so facetiously, they say,
    It stirs the fun right merrily!

XXII.

And now around his festive board,
Groaning with viands that afford
    The amplest proof of taste,
Is seated many a merry guest,
To crack his mirth-provoking jest,
    And break his morning's fast.

XXIII.

For know the Rock House on the Sound,
Is famous all the wide world round,
    For hospitable fare,
And that its landlord, to forestall
The epicurian wants of all,
    Ransacks earth, sea, and air;

XXIV.

And sets his tables groaning forth
With all the luxuries of the North,
    As well as tropic clime;
And all that wealth and taste afford
To grace alike an ample board
    With beauty and with wine.

XXV.

We register our names as follow:—
I, "Peter Snooks, of Snookville Hollow,"
    Mæcenas, "Count D' Esprit,"
And call for twenty things at once,
A brandy smash, a whisky punch,
    A port-wine sangaree;

XXVI.

Two lemonades with "sticks" to match,
Two "cobblers" without awl to scratch;
    Two "snifters" stiff and strong;
Two "stoughtons," and two "brandies straight,"
Two nags with a "two forty" gait,
    To ride the hills among.

XXVII.

For Rock House nags are said to be
As swift of foot as Mercury,
    When wing'd and girded tight,
Or swift as Puck, who, at his birth,
Could put a girdle round the earth,
    In half an hour's flight!

XXVIII.

I pray the " critics" not to stare,
I only speak of Upson's fare;
    What's *said* about his nags,
May or may not be wholly true,
Though if " Young Ed." could put 'em through,
    He'd no doubt take the " rags!"

XXIX.

But whether his nags be fast or slow,
One thing is certainly most true:—
    West Haven "saints" are faster,
And run a more successful race,
If not to win each christian grace,
    At least to win our laughter!

•XXX.

They're always on some rampage high,
Or in some tragic agony,
    In hopes to make their way
To heaven through expiatory grace,
As if the devil had no place
    Reserved for such as they!

XXXI.

Deluded mortals! they shall find
His sooty majesty inclined
    Erelong to do his will;
To shower his tender mercies down
In fire and brimstone through the town,
    And give them all their fill

XXXII.

Of that most dietetic fare,
He has reserved for them in store:—
    To wit, gridiron steaks,
Cut from some tough old grisly bear,
Or from the rump of thief or liar,
    Or other vile ingrates,

XXXIII.

Doomed like Prometheus to be torn
By vulturous beak from night t'll morn,
    And still their flesh renew,
To gratify the insatiate maw
Of wretches that forever gnaw
    At what they can't gnaw through!

XXXIV.

For if beyond the Lethean wave,
West Haven "saints" are not to have
    Their honest dues; why, then
Sheer downright knavery ought to be
Encouraged most emphatically,
    By every poet's pen!

XXXV.

And hanging ought to be set forth
As recompense of honest worth,
    A passport free to heaven ;
Such as the murderer might share
With every culprit, thief, and liar,
    Without a sin forgiven !

XXXVI.

But to my TALE, which ought to be
Continuous with rascality;
    Or rather, to the tangled thread
Of my poetical discourse,
Which runs at random, like a horse
    Too mettlesome to lead!

XXXVII.

Mæcenas and myself have dined,
And what is better still, have " wined;"
    Which put us in such jovial vein,
That one would almost swear who knew us,
'Twas Upson's fare alone that drew us
    From Pluto's realm to earth again.

XXXVIII.

But this were libel on Mæcenas,
As kissing Dido was on Æneas,
    Although the poet swears,
(I mean the Mantuan bard) that they
Kissed through the live-long night, till day
    Swung wide its golden bars!

XXXIX.

And were, besides, a jump too far
At false conclusion; for the war
    That now so desolates the land
With fire and sword and carnage wild,
Where slain on slain promiscuous piled,
    Are seen on every hand,

XL.

Is what first drew us to the shores,
Famed for its literary "bores,"
    And intellectual women
Of the blue-stocking stripe, who share
The burdens of the State, and wear
    All sorts of gear and trimming!

XLI.

For instance, the "coal-scuttle" bonnet,
With flaunting flowers enough upon it
    To cover a prairie over,
And faces dimpling underneath
With smiles like Circe's, fraught with death,
    To unsuspecting lover!

XLII.

And "bloomer," worn by spinster maids,
To palm their drumsticks off for legs
    On some greenhorn or other,
Who never dreampt before to see
Such "sights" of rare "agility"
    Displayed to friend or lover!

XLIII.

But fancied women folks were made,
Like French preserves or marmalade,
    Of sweatmeats rich and rare,
Whose virtues were to be concealed,
Or tasted only when revealed
    At wedding, feast, or fair!

XLIV.

But to my tale. Our dinner through,
We took a stroll a mile or two,
    And came into the town,
Wherein we found a group of people
Inside a church without a steeple,
    Putting "disunion" down!

XLV.

The plan for doing this was new,
Novel, and most ingenious too,
    As few with me will doubt;
It was to keep the church together,
In every kind of wind and weather,
    By keeping "Christians" out!

XLVI.

And to prevent "secession," rule
All members out, however full
    The church might chance to be;
And then appoint an "agent sole,"
With full and absolute control
    Of all church property!

XLVII.

With summary power to bar the doors,
Tear up the carpets from the floors,
    And nail the windows down;
Purloin the plate, the alter rive,
Smash stoves and organ pipes, and drive
    The parson out of town.

XLVIII.

Such powers as these were deemed to be
Essential to church unity;
    And if enforced in season,
Might save the church from every rent
The envious "Cascas" could invent,
    With all their hated "treason"!

XLIX.

It seems the clerk, who read the laws,
Was posted up in all the flaws;
    Especially in this:—
That none could ever member be
Of any church however free,
    Without request of his,

L.

First duly and in writing made,
(Before some legal meeting had,)
    To clerk or clerk *pro tem.*;
And run the gauntlet of a vote,
Or chances of a *nem. con.* note,
    Entered by clerkly pen.

LI.

Discovering this most potent flaw,
Latent or patent in the law,
    This astute christian clerk,
With pious motive, not for pelf,
At once devoutly set himself
    With three M. D's to work!

LII.

The church though small had grown to be
Quite rich in gifts and legacy,
    And hence they all decide
(I mean the clerk and three M. D's)
To keep the records and the keys
    Where none could filch or hide;

LIII.

Or rather none but such as they,
Who could, 'tis said, both filch and pray
    Devoutly for the nonce;
Or wear an equally long face
At shaving notes, or saying grace,
    Or doing both at once.

LIV.

But there was still another "flaw",
Or rather, stubborn fact of law,
    Which made them ill at ease;
And it was this, (the fact I state
To show their case was desperate,)
    The parson had the keys!

LV.

This was a "clincher" to the clerk,
As he had learned from lawyer Quirk,
    The man of quip and flaw;
Who from his musty books had found
Possession, with the keys, was crowned
    As "nine points of the law."

LVI.

But "nothing venture, nothing have",
Was Barnet's motto; so he gave
    Direction to purloin the keys
To Dr. Ames, who chanced to be
The biggest rascal of the three,—
    That is, the three M, D's.

LVII.

But not the biggest of the four,
As you'll admit with me before
    You've read my "Knaviad" through;
For though the doctor's sins were rank
And smelt to heaven, he was frank,
    And true to friend as foe.

LVIII.

Not so with B—n—t. He could smile
On friend or foe with equal guile,
    And stab with equal grace
A christian friend behind his back,
Or heathen foe upon his track,
    If not met face to face.

LIX.

His neighbors often wondered why
He never looked them in the eye,
    And guessed the cause in vain;
For diagnosis would have shown
Them this disease, and this alone—
    Strabismus on *the brain!*

LX.

Or "mental squinting," much the same
As what we see in certain game,
    For instance, in the ounce;
Or in sly reynard, which, pursued
By hound and hunter through the wood,
    Looks forty ways at once!

LXI.

But A----s soon found his task to be
More difficult than either he
    Or B--n--t had surmised,
For parson Z--ll had "smelt the rat,"
Or rather guessed what they were at,
    With all their craft disguised.

LXII.

And so he went, as rumor states,
And of his keys got duplicates,
    To guard against surprise;
And had them safely laid away
Against what's called a "rainy day,"
    In metaphor's disguise.

LXIII.

But time rolled on as time will roll,
When there's no Joshua of old
    To stay its fiery car,
And soon it brought them, in its course,
The appointed hour to rehearse
    The music of the choir.

LXIV.

Forth to the parsonage they go,
The doctor and his "doxies" two,
    All of the choir of course;
And chuckling hugely in their sleeves,
Say to the parson, "By your leaves
    The keys, sir, to rehearse!"

LXV.

The parson blandly hands them to 'em,
(How could he help it, since he knew 'em
    All of the choir to be?)
When, after taking time to sing,
They hand him back his "private" string,
    Minus the church-door key.

LXVI.

"With this adroitly-managed theft,
There's nothing more," says B—n—t, "left
    For *us*, the church, to do;
We've got 'em in the 'nine holes' tight
And now we'll put this lawyer Wr—ht
    And parson Z—ll both through!"

LXVII.

"On Sunday next they'll find the church
Has kindly left them in the lurch,
    With all their gifts of grace;
Without so much as a dormouse
To welcome them within the house,
    So snug we've got the place.

LXVIII.

"H——tsh——n will swear and Wr——ht will curse,
And parson Z——ll do something worse,
    Neglect his daily prayers;
While Mrs. Z. will vent her spleen,
Look daggers at us o'er the green,
    And put on queenly airs!

LXIX.

"Next Sunday morn will see 'em scarce,
Or rather see a downright farce
    Verging on tragic mood;
Some fifty Z——llites tearing mad,
And swearing vengeance on the head
    Of B——n——t and of W——d.

LXX.

" 'Twill be a most stupendous joke,
And how they'll rave, and fume, and choke,
    With their unvented spleen;
'Twould pay for pilgrimage to Rome,
Only to see the Z——llites come
    Next Sunday, on the green."

LXXI.

And B⟨⟩n⟨⟩t rubbed his hands the while,
And grinned a most sardonic smile,
   (Satan might do as much,)
Yes, grinned a "ghastly smile," and swore
He never laughed as much before,
   Inside or out of Church!

LXXII.

It was arranged they all should be
At B⟨⟩n⟨⟩t's house, the farce to see,
   Early on Sunday morn;
And when the hour for church came round,
The knavish conclave all were found
   There, jubilant—"in a horn!"

LXXIII.

For hardly had they got together,
And made their comments on the weather,
   Before they saw the smoke
Go curling from the chimney flue
In merry wreaths, as if it knew
   The purport of their "joke!"

LXXIV.

And then the Church's merry bell
Pealed forth its laughter loud and shrill,
   And made the very air
Sonorous with its mirthful glee,
As if in merriment to see
   The "Jeremy Diddlers" stare!

LXXV.

As stare they did through window pane,
With lowering looks, as o'er the green
    They saw the Z⸺llites go
And enter straight within the door,
Whose lock was never picked before,
    By craft of imp below!

LXXVI.

The doctor's horse tied to a post
In front of B⸺n⸺t's, seemed quite lost,
    Amid the general stare
And wonderment the house was in;
And champed his bit with bitter grin,
    O'er his post-prandial fare!

LXXVII.

And B⸺n⸺t's dog ran yelping forth,
Reflecting all his master's wrath
    'Gainst every cur that past;
And finding nothing else to bite,
Grew fierce and furious at the sight
    Of his own tail at last,

LXXVIII.

Which seizing fast within his teeth,
As some vile thing deserving death,
    He gave it such a gripe,
That, like his master's lengthened laughter,
His tail was curtailed ever after,
    Or vanished out of sight!

LXXIX.

And as the story spread abroad,
The town from end to end guffawed
    Incessantly on Monday;
And grinned a universal grin,
To think how B—n—t's "laugh" came in
    So lacrymose on Sunday!

LXXX.

But every farce must have an end,
As every river has a bend,
    And every youth a "bender;"
And now the clerk decides to call
Another meeting, to make all
    Opposed to them surrender,

LXXXI.

Or " strike their colors " in the fight,
Whether or not within the right;
    And so he posts a call
On all such members, good and true,
As had been "legally" put through,
    To meet at church or hall.

LXXXII.

The day at length arrived, and they,
The astute clerk and M. D's. three,
    Came promptly up to time;
A——s, who'd been chairman once before,
Could find no chair, so took the floor,
    Looking both gruff and grim.

LXXXIII.

He said the meeting wished to know
What parson Z—ll was going to do,
   Resign or keep at work,
Against the wishes of Mc C—ry,
W—d, (seven-by-nine apothecary,)
   H—e, W—n—r, and the clerk!

LXXXIV.

These, with himself, he claimed to be
The church *in toto* and *per se*;
   The rest were mere outsiders,
With no more right to worship there,
Or vote for minister or choir,
   Than other church deriders.

LXXXV.

This little outside fling or slur,
Brought lawyer Wr—ht upon the floor,
   A churchman "clad in mail,"
Who hurled such thundering vollies forth,
Of adjectives and direful wrath,
   As made the "conclave" quail.

LXXXVI.

He told them to their teeth ou'right,
He'd have his rights cost what they might,
   No force should put him down,
Nor artifice nor trickster's tricks,
And if it came to blows and kicks,
   He'd see the thing "tried on."

LXXXVII.

The " conclave" tried, but tried in vain,
To thump him down with heel and cane,
   'Mid cries of "Order," "Order;"
His voice still swept above the din,
And wild confusion they were in,
   As bugle swept the Border,

LXXXVIII.

When furious clansmen, sallying forth,
Scoured those regions of the North
   Where recreant foemen came,
All worthy of an honest glaive;
And not like skulking, coward knave,
   Too dastardly to name.

LXXXIX.

But nothing daunted there he stood,
Confronting B⸺t, A⸺s, and W⸺d,
   As hound confronts a pack
Of prairie wolves—the brindled breed,
Who ravenous and full of greed,
   All honest courage lack.

XC.

For hours, 'tis said, he kept the floor,
And might have kept it many more,
   Or till the crack of doom,
For ought they knew; and so to-turn
The tables on him, they adjourn
   Over to B⸺t's room.

XCI.

The "conclave" gone, order began
To reign in Warsaw; and there ran
    A murmur of applause
Throughout the church to see them go,
And all cried out, "Good riddance to
    The marplots and their cause."

XCII.

The shuffling knaves gone from the pack,
The church once more may welcome back
    Her former christian graces;
No choir to giggle during prayers,
No Dr. A——s to smoke cigars
    Or make up monkey faces,

XCIII.

No loud "ahems!" when members went
To kneel at holy sacrament,
    No peering through a hat,
Nor greeting of the Bishop's prayer
For Peace and Union, with the sneer—
    "Never amen to that!"

XCIV.

Such vile disturbances as these,
Approved of in the galleries
    By B——tt, W——d, and others,
Were straightway trumpeted abroad,
To show how Z——ll must be abhored
    By all his christian brothers!

XCV.

'Tis said a vain and stupid ass
Once for a lion tried to pass,
    The monarch of the plain,
And so he got a lion's skin
To wrap his valliant carcass in,
    And brayed with might and main.

XCVI.

But the imposter was no doubt
Known by his long ears peering out;
    So with the knaves I mention,
Who stole the livery of the court
Of heaven, as a last resort,
    To serve the devil in!

XCVII.

But here the Muse would improvise
A strain or two on H—tt—e I—s,
    The doctor's famed *soprano*,
Or rather on the famous choir
In which she giggled during prayer,
    'Mid fumes of rank *Habano*.

XCVIII.

Hark! the music, how they snort it!
Duet, trio, quintet, quartet,
    All in one tremendous wave;
Voices quivering, voices quavering,
Voices trembling, voices shaking,
    All up and down the stave!

XCIX.

How they now relieve their throats
Of their nasal-twanging notes,
    Ye gods! what music flows!
Enough to make one "soar away
To rapture and eternal day,"
    'Mid their ecstatic throes!

C.

Oh, ye shades of Haydn, Mozart!
Yours was but a vulgar prose-art,
    When compared to theirs;
With diminished heads knock under
To the more harmonious thunder
    Of Dr. A——s's choirs!

CI.

But the muse has no desire
To exhaust her treasured fire
    On Beethoevens here;
She would rather make a dash on
Something more in vogue or fashion,
    For this humbug year.

CII.

For instance, on a certain "vile
Apothecary," full of bile,
    Lampooned by "honest Will,"
I mean Will Shakespeare, in whose muse
All rascals get their honest dues,
    And get them to their fill.

CIII.

This nostrum vender, it is said,
For honest inventory, had
    "A beggarly account
Of empty boxes," labelled over
With scraps of Latin, just to cover
    Their emptiness about!

CIV.

And was withal, lean, lank, and shriveled,
And what was more, a little driveled
    About his upper story,
Or in his "attic;" though his tongue
Was on a perfect swivel hung,
    And ran to oratory!

CV.

He used to talk so wondrous wise,
Use words of such equestrian size,
    And look withal so grim,
The common people stood agape
In wonder that his "pericarp"
    Contained so much within!

CVI.

And yet, 'tis said, his brains ran forth
In empty nothings—nothing worth;
    Or ambled like a nag
That has the spring-halt "on the brain,"
Or in each limb and joint the same
    As in each limping leg!

CVII.

Some envious neighbors here and there,
Familiar with this "Shakespeare rare,"
   And with his *avis rare*,
Would point to one of Z—ll's chief foes,
And say within themselves, there goes
   That "vile apothecary!"

CVIII.

But to return. The meeting through,
It was arranged, and that in view
   Of sundry thefts committed,
To keep a cautious watch that night,
And see that every thing was "right,"
   Or rather duly (*W*) *righted!*

CIX.

So they appointed a committee,
And forthwith sent into the city,
   To get a lock and key,
With which to make the church door fast,
Against each arrant knave that past,
   In quest of robbery!

CX.

But while at this, the "agent sole"
Came down "like wolf upon the fold,"
   And ordered all to leave
The church forthwith, or have their meed
Of law and warrant visited
   Upon them, past retrieve!

CXI.

As law nor warrant he had none,
They promptly bid him to be gone,
    But showed him first the door;
And when the "agent sole" went forth,
The "church" from out the church, in **wrath**,
    He threatened all the more.

CXII.

And soon returned with Dr. Allis,
Holding new penalties and pains
    O'er each recusant head,
Demanding "seizin" of his own,
Since he comprised the church alone,
    As "agent aforesaid!"

CXIII.

Hutchison he laughed, and Wright he looked,
As if in "seizin" he was booked,
    And jokingly replied,
If Burnett was the church alone,
The church outside the church they'd **turn**,
    And see what was inside!

CXIV.

Night's sable dragons soon came **down**
To swart the air about the town,
    And revel in its gloom;
To close the eye-lids of the day,
Seal up the past eternity,
    Or bide the crack of doom.

CXV.

Within the church, whose solemn nave
Had neither arch nor architrave,
    Nor spire nor dome for cover,
Three persons sat the long night through,
The one to watch the other two,
    The two to watch the other.

CXVI.

These three were Ba̱r̲n̲t̲t, A̱e̲s, and Wr̲h̲t,
Whose deeds of choler to indite
    The Muse will now proceed,
Though of material she has none
But what "Dame Rumor" seized upon,
    As through the town she sped.

CXVII.

A̱e̲s, freed from matrimonial halter,
Seeks refuge first within the altar,
    Then barricades the door;
While Wr—ht, as if to show his spunk,
Extemporizes, first a "bunk,"
    And then, lays down to snore!

CXVIII.

Meanwhile the " church " or " agent sole, "
Goes forth to skirmish or patrol
    His parish precincts through,
In hopes, with aid of boy and horse,
To rally forth sufficient force
    To force Wr̲ht from his pew.

CXIX.

But first (the fact I ought to mention,)
His "burning" coal-pit needs attention;
    So forthwith he essays
To smother the fires the pit within,
But not the fires that fire him,
    And set him all a-blaze!

CXX.

And after having squelched the flames
Within the pit, he thought of A——s,
    And then of Dr. W——d,
And somehow coupled in his mind
All three together, as you bind
    A tense to varying mood!

CXXI.

And then he thought—the night was dark—
How mad and fiercely rose each spark
    From out his pit on fire;
How blue the flames, and how malign
The light they gave, and then, in fine,
    He thought of his own ire!

CXXII.

And wondered if the fiends below
Had any thing at all to do
    With this night's work of theirs;
And here his dog set up a howl,
As if some dismal ghost or ghoul
    Were flaying both his ears!

CXXIII.

He found his knees were getting weak,
And when he mustered strength to speak
    At length to his own cur,
His tongue was absolutely glued
Between his lips, and like his blood
    Seemed powerless to stir!

CXXIV.

But he returns at length to find
The doctor watering his mind
    With consecrated grape,
Which he, no doubt, had taken freely,
To judge him from his really reely,
    'Locomotive state!

CXXV.

It seems the doctor felt quite sure
Of wine behind the vestry door,
    Within the parson's cupboard;
And hoping not to find it "bare,"
Or void of all intrinsic fare,
    As did "Old Mother Hubbard,"

CVXXI.

The famous one she looked into;
He promptly smashed the cupboard through,
    And lo! there met his eye
Two jolly dimijohns quite full,
At which he took a lengthened pull,
    Or "swig upon the sly."

CXXVII.

And now they crack their stalest jokes
On Z—ll and sundry other folks,
    Especially on Wright,
Whom they could represent full well
As being the "sleepy sentinel,"
    Upon that wakeful night.

CXXVIII.

At this stale joke, Wright gives a snore
That shakes the rafters, to ignore
    His truly wakeful state ;
Then, to suppress his laughter, blows
A blast terrific from his nose,
    Their mirth to irrigate !

CXXIX.

A while thus spent, and Dr. W—d
Drops in to see what state the feud,
    Or church broil, might be in ;
And ratling of a " yarn" or two
Of his own manufacture, threw
    Himself into a grin.

CXXX.

If grin it might be called that drew
His face into a rat-tailed screw,
    Less round perhaps than thin ;
And made him look for all the world,
As if a monkey's tail were quirled,
    In spirals, round his chin !

CXXXI.

The doctor's stay was short and brief;
He had no doubt a vague belief
    There'd be a bloody fight;
And so he tore himself away,
To fight prehaps another day,
    But not upon that night.

CXXXII.

This "brave apothecary" gone,
Barnett and Allis are left alone,
    With Wright, the seventh doser;
And though they plan on plan propose
To thrust him forth, or tweak his nose,
    Each plan but proves a "poser."

CXXXIII.

Allis swears he's armed up to his teeth,
With dirks, revolvers, knives and death,
    And thinks his sleep a sham;
A lure to lead to bloody brawl,
Or possibly to his own fall
    By punctured diaphragm!

CXXXIV.

He thinks the "agent" ought to try
To raise "recruits," or send a spy
    Into his "bunk" or camp,
And seize all weapons "contraband
Of war" that he may have on hand,
    And "confiscate" the scamp!

CXXXV.

But as the fate of every spy
Is death by halter, Haman-high,
    They both declined to go
Within his camp, but hit the plan
Of "forced conscription" to a man,
    The parish precincts through!

CXXXVI.

So Barnet scours the parish wide,
From Painter's Rocks to "Dew-Drop" side,
    But scours, alas, in vain!
For as in love, so those in war,
Once hoisted with their own *petard*,
    Refuse to fight again.

CXXXVII.

After a fruitless night half spent
Upon the errand he was bent,
    The "church" returns at last;
And getting down from off its crupper,
Gets up a *reverent* oyster supper,
    For Ames and its repast!

CXXXVIII.

This, being reverently brought
Where no live oyster ever thought
    Of being brought before,
(To wit, within the chancel,) they,
The "church" and Ames, gulp down, and say,
    "By heavens! how Wright *does* snore!

CXXXIX.

As snore he did with might and main,
Since playing " possum " was his game
    With knaves, in church, or out ;
And when the first faint streaks of day
Revealed the game that they would play,
    His " possum " eyes were shut!

CXL.

Failing to get the aid they sought
Within the church to help them out,
    They go to parson Bryan,
Or rather to his church, and get
Two " bullies," square-built and thick-set,
    Their strength their foe to try on!

CXLI.

Seeing this " bully " force arrayed
Within the church, Wright undismayed
    Arose from out his " bunk ;"
Yet for a moment rubbed his eyes,
As if quite taken by surprise,
    Or " slightually " drunk!

CXLII.

And then he drew from out his pocket
A knife with a tremendous socket,
    Yet more tremendous blade ;
And coolly picked his teeth, to show
The uses it could be put to
    In peace, as bloody raid!

CXLIII.

The "church" now takes another tack,
Resolves itself, itself to sack,
    Or gut from stem to stern;
And seizing every thing in sight,
In way of movables, but Wright,
    The church outside they turn!

CXLIV.

So having cleared the church at last,
And nailed the windows tight and fast,
    And the old organ smashed;
They undertake to try their strength
Upon the stalwart Wright at length,
    Whose eyes indignant flashed.

CXLV.

Within the vestibule he stood
In sullen, grim, and wrathful mood,
    And eyed his foes askance;
Deeming the five but half a match
In any honest fight or scratch,
    Where "science" had a chance!

CXLVI.

But he no doubt mistook their aim,
In fancying "bully" Ward was "game,"
    For the first blow he gave
Was "foul," as any knave would swear,
Who e'er saw fight at "Donnie Fair,"
    Or wore an honest glaive!

CXLVII.

Instead of sparring for the nonce;
Like "loons" they all pitched in at once,
    Which made him still more wroth,
And when they seized him by the hair,
It no doubt made him rip and swear
    A most unchristian oath!

CXLVIII.

The fight waxed furiously at last;
Heels flew in air, and blows fell fast,
    And louder grew the din;
Twas evident a storm was brewing,
Potent alike of wrath and ruin,
    That gray old church within!

CXLIX.

But every contest has its close
When once it comes to direful blows,
    What e'er its end or aim;
Though five to one is such a tussle,
Was rather shabbier proof of muscle,
    Than some might care to claim!

CL.

And now the story of the fight
Goes forth in colors all bedight,
    And flies from door to door;
Each rumor follows rumor's track,
And in its turn comes hurrying back
    With fifty rumors more!

CLI.

As when a patient chanced to throw
Up something once just like a crow,
 In color—not in feather,
Forthwith from house to house it flew
That he had vomited up two
 Prodigious crows together!

CLII.

So now the story flew abroad
That Wr—ht had flogged the "bully" W**a**r**d**,
 And half a dozen more;
And from the *nave* within the church,
Had given all the *knaves* the lurch,
 By bolting through the door!

CLIII.

That, with his spectacles on nose,
He dealt such furious, blinding blows
 Upon each separate sconce,
That they went staggering o'er the green,
As if their dubious eyes had seen
 A thousand stars at once!

CLIV.

But this no doubt exaggerates
As to the blows upon their pates,
 For they could never bear it;
Although 'tis true, when Wr—ht first threw
His *left* at "bully" W**a**r**d**, he drew
 Full half a mug of claret!

CLV.

But this was not so "foul" a blow
As that which knocked the cupboard through,
    The very night before;
Nor was it quite so foul a crime
As guzzling consecrated wine
    Behind the vestry door!

CLVI.

This skrimmage over, parson Z—ll
Writes to the Bishop what befell
    His church upon that night;
Imploring him, by all that's good,
To visit his vile neighborhood,
    And "exorcise" it quite!

CLVII.

The "conclave" also write to know
If B—n—t, or their "church," can't do
    Whatever their church pleases;
And seem to be in quite a huff,
To think when B—n—t takes his snuff,
    'Tis not the church that sneezes!

CLVIII.

The Bishop hastens to report,
That he'll immediately resort
    To this recusant charge,
With four Assessors to decide
What they shall do, by what abide,
    In church affairs at large.

CLIX.

The day appointed, he arrives,
And takes the "church" quite by surprise,
    As he demands the keys
And all church muniments, to show
That B—n—t and the church are two,
    In his, the Bishop's eyes.

CLX.

He brings along Assessors four,
All grave and reverend, with the power
    To sit with him and try
This "case," so knotty and so full
Of "legal" points, that one might pull
    A hundred o'er each eye!

CLXI.

Two doctors and two reverends, from
The nearest or adjacent town,
    Make up the board of triers;
Their names I ought perhaps to state,
To make the record as complete
    As history requires!

CLXII.

B——dsl—y, Ha—w——d, Dr—n and B——sh—r,
All quite reverend and used to
    Questions vexed and knotty,
Sit with the Bishop, reverend seignior,
In lofty, sad, yet stern demeanor,
    On this case so "spotty

CLXIII.

And leprous" with disease and death,
To all church increase, life, and wealth,
  As well as christian graces;
And for six mortal hours, they
Question, deliberate, and pray,
  With fixed, repellant faces!

CLXIV.

They sternly question B⸺n⸺t first,
And wish to know what "fiend accurst"
  Inspired this deadly feud;
He, slinking down into his boots,
With voice scarce audible, deputes
  For speaker—Dr. W⸺d!

CLXV.

The doctor tries to state their case,
But "brings up" in a wild-goose chase,
  Or helter-skelter ramble;
A kind of mental steeple-chasing,
Where horses "of all sorts" are racing
  In one wild skimble-skamble!

CLXVI.

'Tis "point all no point" in his mind,
Or mental labor of that kind,
  Lampooned in fable nice,
Showing how hard the mountains strain,
And how prolific is their pain,
  When they give birth to mice!

CLXVII.

Of parson Z—ll he speaks quite chary,
Yet claims to be as really sorry
    To part with him as any;
He's liked him long, and *would* like longer,
If he was what he should be—younger,
    With all his gifts so many.

CLXVIII.

An upright, stainless life he led,
A christian both in word and deed,
    A man who lived for heaven;
But, as a preacher, quite too slow
For certain "fast" ones here below,
    By devil "*in tandem*" driven!

CLXIX.

For in this age of fire and smoke,
A man must strike a mightier stroke
    Than e'er old Vulcan did,
And forge a bolt to hurl at sin,
Louder and hotter than all within
    The bowels of Ætna hid!

CLXX.

To *save* a soul is not enough;
Man's vengeance is of sterner stuff,
    He makes a hell of fire,
And down its liquid crata hurls
The victims of a thousand worlds,
    To gratify his ire!

CLXXI.

Why, then, should not good parson Z–ll
Extemporize a half-way hell,
   For those who live too " slow,"
Who do not put away their wives,
Or play the wanton like Miss ――
   With every grass-fed beau !

CLXXII.

Who do not show themselves to be
Experts in all rascality,
   Liars on every tack ;
Professing friendship to the face,
Yet stabbing with a christian grace
   Behind each christian back !

CLXXIII.

Who do not grasp at every dime
The widow holds against such time
   As she may make her will ;
Or curse the clergyman who gave
Such timely warning as to save
   The purse of widow ―― !

CLXXIV.

Who do not drive " two forty " nags,
And run against all proper " snags"
   In journeying their lives through ;
Who do not " high old rampage " have
At times, with wine and *nymphs de pave*,
   As all " crack " fellows do !

CLXXV.

Who do not talk of "honor bright,"
Yet put all honor out of sight
    The moment honor's due;
And boast of "honest triumphs" had
With unsophisticated maid,
    As beautiful as true!

CLXXVI.

Who do not pick an honest purse,
At dice or cards, or something worse,
    When their exchequer's low;
Or make their "governors" come down
At proper times with their last crown,
    Their proper *love* to show!

CLXXVII.

Such "sloth" as this shows little grace,
In such a purely christian place
    As this is said to be,
And argues want of christian "blood,"
And that most mettlesome of food—
    Fresh bivalves from the sea!

CLXXVIII.

And then, 'tis said, the parson's daughter
Got married as she "had'nt ought to,"
    In the old fashioned way,
To one she really loved, and not
To one she merely meant to "spot"
    Upon his wedding day.

CLXXIX.

In doing this, she'd really given
A bad example to West Haven,
    That might contagious prove,
And lead some unsophisticated,
Shallow maidens, to get mated
    To those they truly love!

CLXXX.

We all can see that this would lead
To consequences grave indeed,
    Since disobedient daughters
Might first impose upon the State
Expenses ruinously great
    By multiplying paupers,

CLXXXI.

And then subject our needy church,
To be once more left in the lurch
    For want of funds to carry;
And all because these daughters choose
Their "opportunities" to loose
    When they decide to marry!

CLXXXII.

Not that Miss Z. had married poor,
Or mated with a "country boor;"
    It quite the contrary proved,
But she defiantly had dared
To marry, as her future "laird,"
    One whom she really loved!

CLXXXIII.

This was her great offence—too great
To be forgiven by church or state,
   In their most potent need
Of funds to fill contractor's purses;
And hence, the direful, bitter curses
   Now heaped upon her head.

CLXXXIV.

Oh, age of folly—age of gold!
To see your daughters bought and sold
   Like Ethiopean slave!
Just to replete an empty purse,
Or what is infinitely worse—
   Consign them to their grave!

CLXXXV.

Or rather to their living tomb,
Where light of heaven shall never come,
   Nor love shall ever bless,
But hate, eternal hate, preside,
In all her rankling state of pride,
   As well as bitterness!

CLXXXVI.

But to return to W—d's discourse;
No case was ever stated worse,
   Or half so lamely put;
He cut and haggled it throughout,
As one who maladroitly sought
   To hide a cloven foot!

CLXXXVII.

'Twas all the reverend gents. could do
To keep their faces reverent through
    The harrangue, or thereafter;
And when he finished up at last,
They bit their lips to keep them fast,
    Against a burst of laughter!.

CLXXXVIII.

The case upon the other side,
Was briefly this: They all had tried,
    But tried in vain, to get
Their legal rights, and now they brought
Their case before the Assessor's Court,
    To have it squarely met.

CLXXXIX.

The church at least were five to one
In favor of still going on
    Without a charge of *role*,
And *hence*, the only point, if any,
Was who should rule, the few or many,
    The church or " agent sole."

CXC.

The Assessors now the case review,
And manage after an hour or two,
    To bring in their report;
In which they happily decide
The point, " 'twixt north and northeast side,"
    And cut the gordian knot!

CXCI.

That is to say, they first condemn
All that the "conclave" did, and then
    Endorse all they had done;
And as a *salvo*, then invite
The many who are in the right,
    To gracefully succumb!

CXCII.

The friends of Z—ll looked blank and grum,
And thought it very like a hum.
    Or more like splitting hairs,
Though splint of hair they could'nt see
'Twixt tweedledum and tweedledee,
    As did the reverend triers!

CXCIII.

But they decide a little further,
As separating this from t'other,
    That parson Z—ll must not
Recall his resignation made,
But have his salary all paid
    To Easter on the spot.

CXCIV.

And this was to be raised in full
By contribution from the whole—
    His friends as well as foes;
With power to do it by committee,
Selected from the town or city,
    As they, the whole, might choose!

CXCV.

But it so happened that the " whole "
Decided, if the power to rule
    Was only in the " few,"
They'd let the " said committee " slide
And leave the rulers to provide
    The salary now due!

CXCVI.

And to these rulers, it is said,
Each one advances, first a "red,"
    To answer the award;
And then advises them to see
The balance raised immediately,
    As times are getting hard!

CXCVII.

The balance comes like pulling teeth,
Or rather like a lingering death,
    When life is in its noon;
And makes the purse and wallet groan,
As when some reckless spendthrift's **drawn**
    On his last picayune!

CXCVIII.

Some wondered why the award was **made**
So very like a masquerade,
    Or fancy ball in town;
With all its phases so complete
That neither side could really " see 't, "
    Or gulp the thing quite down!

CXCIX.

But rumor had it, (no one knew
Exactly whence it sprung or grew,)
    That Dr. B. had made it
With such a Machiavellian pen,
That Z—ll would get his money, when
    The " few " had really paid it!

CC.

And rumor had it further blown,
In sundry circles, through the town,
    That Dr. B. had tried,
By laboring with his colleagues hard,
To get the principal award
    Set finally aside;

CCI.

In order to releive the " few "
From any further brawl or stew
    With the recusant " many,"
And recognize the " agent sole "
As having all in his control,
    Since he controlled the money!

CCII.

For money had become of late,
The only lever in church or state;
    And nothing could be worse,
Than simply having " brains " to glut
An empty stomach, or to put
    Quietus on a purse!

CCIII.

Though "brains" might answer very well
For one who lived, like parson Z—ll,
    In country town or village;
But in a city big with show,
,Twas money made the "Doctor" go.
    As army goes by pillage!

CCIV.

For money is the almighty *nexus*
In church and state, from Maine to Texas,
    And if the "few" can not
Have their own way in church affairs,
No matter what its grace or prayers,
    The church must go to pot!

CCV.

Time was when "brains" might win the race,
In building up a church like this,
    Against the "almighty dollar,"
But now, by general assumption,
The dollar, superceeding gumption,
    Leaves "cannie brains" to follow.

CCVI.

These arguments addroitly made,
Almost persuaded it is said,
    The Bishop to knock under;
But one Assessor, parson Dr—n,
Indignantly put his foot down,
    And "would'nt—no, by thunder!"

CCVII.

The "few" were then advised to take
Another, or a legal tack,
    And set themselves at work
To get the church *in statu quo*,
Or on such footing as to go
    By aid of lawyer Quirk.

CCVIII.

It seems there happened once to be
Up in old, ancient Bethany,
    A church that did'nt know,
Exactly when the time came round
For them to gather in the town
    And put election through,

CCIX.

That is, within the church; and so
They let the election fall quite through,
    A *casus omissus* good;
When all agreed to go to court
In order to get out their "foot"
    The quickest way the could.

CCX.

The court decides, (as courts will do,
When they their learning wish to show)
    The case both wrong and right;
'Twas wrong to let election slip,
But right to have no rivalship,
    In view of their sad plight!

CCXI.

And so they beat the legal cover,
And hold that vestries may hold over,
    As well as church committees,
When there has been so clear a case
Of church omission, as took place
    Among these worthy laities!

CCXII.

Now lawyer Quirk sees in this case,
A precedent of "special grace,"
    For all this church's broil;
They might go back a year or two,
And all they'd done, at once undo,
    And thus the "many" foil!

CCXIII.

An old committee, long since dead,
Might be raked up, though much decayed,
    And in bad odor still,
To take the place of those elected
The year before, but who'd neglected
    Their proper place to fill,

CCXIV.

And this would knock the corner stone
From underneath what they had done,
    The Bishop and Assessors,
In holding that the "many" were
In membership established clear,
    As well as church professors,

CCXV.

And finally, on Easter day,
In "eighteen-hundred sixty-three,
    They galvanize the dead,
Defunct old vestry, who come forth
From out their mummy cases, wroth
    At being thus beshred!

CCXVI.

But wheedling them into belief,
That they had really come to life,
    And were no longer mummies,
They get them to put forth a call,
For a church meeting annual,—
    I mean these three church dummies.

CCXVII.

The meeting called, the "few" convene;
The "many" are no longer seen
    To pant for broil or fray;
The "conclave" has the amplest swing,
With not a soul on them to bring
    Confusion or dismay.

CCXVIII.

The church's walls look stained and bare,
The stoves are neither here nor there,
    The altar cloth is gone,
And cobwebs from the farthest end
Of musty ceiling, now depend,
    With spiders hanging on!

CCXIX.

The empty desk, in looking down
Upon the "agent," seems to frown;
    The organ seems to say,
Where are my smashed and broken pipes,
And whence those villainous "wipes"
    I got upon that day,

CCXX.

When you, the church's "agent sole,"
Came down like wolf upon my fold,
    And drove them hence for aye?
And *you* a churchman, good and true,
Out on your miserable crew
    Forever and a day!

CCXXI.

The outraged organ speaks in vain,
Their deafened ears and hearts to gain;
    They set themselves at work,
And as if bent on hellish prize,
In spite of organ, organize
    Themselves into a church!

CCXXII.

Their work is ended,—so they think;
The deed is entered black with ink,
    But blacker with intent;
Some thirty members stricken from
The church's fold, to give them room,
    Or give their spleen a vent!

CCXXIII.

And spleen they had more splenetic
Than ever hypochondriac,
   Or spleeny mortal had;
With tongues that dripped with worse saliva
Than ever mad dog's tooth could slaver,
   However deadly mad!

CCXXIV.

But then, *their* spleen was not enough,
And so they sought for spleenier stuff—
   An old maid's withered tongue,
That could a little louder *bawl* (*yell*),
Exude worse venom, or worse gall,
   And more incessant run!

CCXXV.

This "withered tongue," 'tis said, went forth
Throughout the parish, charged with wrath
   And venom on the head
Of parson Z—ll, and on all those
Who did not ministration choose
   Less suited to their need!

CCXXVI.

Their work is ended;—so 'tis said,
And all their wrath is visited,
   In vials doubly full,
Upon this christian church, that they,
The "few," may have supremacy,
   In what they call church rule!

CCXXVII.

Their work is ended :—yet, how true
It is, that villainy falls through
    The very pit it makes;
And that ill deeds come home to roost,
When we have calculated most
    On setting fast our stakes!

CCXXVIII.

Their work is ended :—oh, how few
Will ever find such saying true!
    No work doth ever end;
That of to-day lives on to morrow,
And either brings its joy or sorrow,
    As kindred work shall tend!

CCXXIX.

No, 'tis not ended; this to say,
Were bitterest piece of irony,
    On all the " conclave " did ;
They tried to make perpetual
The strife the Bishop tried to heal,
    And in his anger chid.

CCXXX.

And now his stern command that they
Should strictly his award obey,
    Is flouted to his teeth;
While brooding o'er the church is hung
A pall of spiritual gloom,
    Next to the second death.

CCXXXI.

The Muse would still prolong her strain,
But begs Euterpe's fire in vain,
    For more extended flight;
She only gives her *lash*—not fire,
When knaves invoke her special ire
    Upon their heads to light!

CCXXXII.

But at some future time, she may
Vouchsafe me all I ask to-day,—
    Her most indignant flame,
To light the altar of my verse
With words as fierce, and thoughts as terse,
    As fiery epigram.

CCXXXIII.

Meanwhile, I'll wait to see if they
Take the poetic lash to-day
    In anger less than sorrow;
Or whether they seek, with looks morose,
To catch another and tougher dose
    Administered to-morrow!

CCXXXIV.

Thus ends my "Knaviad" on the church:—
But I must not leave in the lurch
    Its chairman—Dr. Adams;
He's done his dirty work for Barnett,
And now I'll touch him up with sonnet,
    And labor for his pains!

CCXXXV.

I'll take him at the close of day:—
Good parson Z^e-ll has gone to pray,
 And sacrament dispense
To dying neighbor, near her end,
Whose symptoms, each and all, portend
 A speedy exit hence!

CCXXXVI.

'Tis near this self same "chairman's" door:—
A sabbath evening, just before
 The eyelids of God's holy day
Were closed in slumber, and he felt—
This godly parson—as he knelt,
 How good it was to pray,

CCXXXVII.

Especially with one so soon
To go before the Great Unknown,
 The I Am of the skies;
Whose great commission he had borne
So many years within that town,
 Dispensing charities.

CCXXXVIII

He pours his soul to God in trust:—
"Eternal Father! if it *must*
 Be as our fears foredoom,
Oh, take thine humble handmaid here,
And bear her upward, where nor tear
 Nor sorrow e'er shall come!"

CCXXXIX

And though the christian now revives,
Her soul still craves the upper skies,
    Longs to depart in peace;
Yet earthly wishes too are there,
Devoutly hallowing the prayer,
    That death may not release

CCXL.

The loved one from her bondage yet;
And so she lingers to beget
    Alternate hope and fear;
And when at length some annodyne
Is wanted, or domestic wine,
    The parson seeks it near.

CCXLI.

Thoughtless at such a time, if any,
Of danger from the " few " or " many,"
    He seeks the nearest door,
Imploring some quick cordial there,
If they had any such to spare,
    The dying to restore.

CCXLII.

A—s sees the godly man approach,
And madly leaping from his coach,
    In which he'd driven home,
Seizes a piece of broken felly,
And swears he'll smash his head to jelly,
    If he's not quickly gone.

CCXLIII.

But nothing daunted, in he goes
Amid a threatened shower of blows,
    And makes his errand good;
Here noble sire and dastard son
Confront each other, man to none,
    And thus is quelled his blood.

CCXLIV.

But not before the wretch is able
To hurl some dishes from the table,
    That graze the parson's face;
The act of coward, double-dyed,
Since priestly hands are doubly tied
    By precept and by grace.

CCXLV.

And oh, ye gods of lofty Rome!
On whom this christian world looks down
    With such supreme disdain,
Had there been sinner such as A——s,
Within your sacred temples' fanes
    Hades had belched again!—

CCXLVI.

Had vomited its fiercest fire
Into old Rome's poluted air,
    And made the welkin ring
With fiendish clamors for the knave,
Who such impiety could brave,
    Or such dishonor bring!

CCXLVII.

And then this "doctor" (few may know it)
Figured quite largely as a poet,
 Lampooning parson Z—ll.
Without one grain of sense or wit
In all the wretched trash he writ,
 So vile his doggerel!

CCXLVIII.

As Mævius once, in ancient Rome,
Whom neither gods nor man would crown
 With the first sprig of bay,
Voided his wretched, riff-raff rhymes,
Or gallimaufry on the times
 And men of his own day,

CCXLIX.

So now, this poetizing ass,
With more than Mævian front and brass,
 Attempts to void his trash
And runs about the town to tell
How he has flayed the parson Z—ll,
 With his poetic lash!

CCL.

Write on! a glorious age for rhyme,
Thou brainless ass of modern time!
 Ay, go it stiff and strong!
Incumbent on thy filmy wing,
Still hold thy flight, still deign to sing,
 Thou jackanapes of song!

CCLI.

And when you've finished up your rhymes,
Go forth and chronicle your crimes
    Unblushingly in prose;
Tell all your cronies how you brought
Your wife to seek divorce in court,
    And what she did depose.

CCLII.

And though it blast your eye-balls, read
The damning record that is spread
    Upon the files in court;
Then go and hang yourself as high
As Haman hung, when Mordecai
    Escaped the noose he wrought!

CCLIII.

But speaking of this Haman's noose,
Reminds me sadly of the use
    It might have been put to!
Even in those barbaric times,
Ere virtues ranked as highest crimes,
    Or crimes to virtues grew.

CCLIV.

It might have tied up Haman's tongue,
With all its slanders, or have wrung
    The gall from out his liver;
And left the matrons of that day
Less tittle-tattle when at tea,
    To shoot from venom's quiver.

CCLV.

Our age had seen more mirth than jesters,
Our homes less Vashtis and more Esthers,
   Had king Ahasuerus
Not got so merry once with wine,
After a seven day's feast or dine,
   As to grow comic-serious!

CCLVI.

But then, our modern Vashtis marry,
In all respects, no doubt, as chary,
   As was this ancient queen!
And would, like her, withhold their beauty,
At court or banquet, as a duty,
   Though dying to be seen!

CCLVII.

I speak of what I know of those
Who tweak their liege-lords by the nose,
   On every state occasion,
And "wear the breeches," as we say,
In vulgar parlance of the day,
   Without a hair's abrasion!

CCLVIII.

Who marry to get rid at once,
Of husband, lover, loon and dunce,
   All in one category,
Without restraint upon them after,
Except small scandal and much laughter,
   In circles amatory!

CCLIX.

'Tis said some cases in West Haven
Might with great pungency be given.
    In certain high-bred quarters;
But then 'twere strange this were not said,
Since scandal never goes to bed
    Except with Eve's fair daughters.

CCLX.

Nor ever closes there an eye.
But keeps a watch continually—
    This Argus, hundred-eared;
Hoping to catch some rumor vile,
Afloat in dreams, or borne on smile,
    Or accents scarcely heard!

CCLXI.

But I'll not " mill" this scandal, though
I mean to put all scandal through
    The *mill* before I'm done,
And furnish forth a "grist" to those
Who scour the streets with blistered toes.
    To blister with their tongue!

CCLXII.

There's Mrs. Pryint—you may know her—
And Mrs. Tipton, scarce below her,
    In wealth and high "posish;"
They're both such greedy scandal-mongers,
That one for scandal never hungers
    But t'other serves a dish!

CCLXIII.

And the Miss Galls, with blistering tongue,
Old maids that want their withers wrung,
   To judge them from their tether;
Who from the cup of scandal sip,
And with their snuff-bags sit and "dip,"
   Whilst they malign together!

CCLXIV.

And Mrs. Gangrene, from whose tongue
Continual festers drip and run,
   Or gather but to break,
In thicker volume, on the head
Of some poor neighbor, too ill-bred
   Her husband to hen-peck!

CCLXV.

And Mrs. Wormwood, whom to taste
Would be like condiment or paste,
   Made of the flowers of rue;
Who, to her husband grown morose,
Gives tongue-wort, in continuous dose,
   To put the poor man through!

CCLXVI.

And Mrs. Virjuice, green-eyed dame,
(Her spectacles are much the same
   In color as her eyes,)
Who keeps a look-out for new comers,
And post-haste gathers up all rumors,
   About them, as they rise!

CCLXVII.

And Mrs. Grimface, galled and jaded,
And what annoys her most—quite faded,
    Who lives in that new house,
And gives a party once a quarter
To show herself off, not her daughter,
    Or amiable spouse!

CCLXVIII.

And Mrs. Primrose, starched all over,
As one would baste a snipe or plover,
    And looking each year better;
Her husband's gone so much from home,
She'd no doubt "gorge herself in gloom,"
    If other men would let her!

CCLXIX.

And Mrs. Vindex, who can throw
The smallest kind of pebble through
    Each vitreous house in town,
And gather "motes" from neighbor's eyes,
Without remotest thought to seize
    The "beam" within her own!

CCLXX.

These several dames, each in their way,
"Cream up" our aristocracy
    With their incipient butter,
And save it, first from being lammed,
And then incontinently damned,
    Or thrust into the gutter.

CCLXXI.

For know, kind reader, there can be
No smaller aristocracy
    In any town or city,
Than what we've got among us here,
In what is called a certain " sphere,"
    By jesters nice and witty.

CCLXXII.

In origin they claim to come
From ancient stock within the town,
    Some lordly bivalve-vender,
Or " oysterman," in common phrase,
Who once a week, 'tis said, said grace,
    And then went on a " bender,"

CCLXXIII.

Or from some daring navigator
Who took the " bar " for the equator,
    And navigated round,
In various bays and inlets wide,
From Oyster river to Fort Hale side,
    But never crossed the sound!

CCLXXIV.

Who once, 'tis said, got cast away
Near " Grape Vine Point," up in the bay,
    In manner bold and risky;
But when the facts were known, 'twas found
He'd only run his craft aground
    Upon a — jug of whisky!

CCLXXV.

These daring "navigators" had
Originally taken shad
    Between the bridge's tressles;
But when the shad gave out, they turned
Their nets adrift, and thenceforth earned
    Their bread by bagging muscles!

CCLXXVI.

This proved a dangerous kind of "sailing,"
And caused no doubt much grief and wailing
    Among their several spouses,
Who saw them "under bare poles" scud,
And often founder in the mud,
    With fearful loss of — trowsers!

CCLXXVII.

They were a jolly set of tars,
Those rare old clammers on the bars,
    With rake and hoe and shovel;
And who would not most *clamorous* be
In praise of such an ancestry,
    Though sprung from lowliest hovel!

CCLXXVIII.

Yet strange to say, their sons have come
On all such "jolly tars" to frown,
    As if they thought to say:—
Your presence is offensive, sir,
It galls my wife, suggests to her,
    What I had been to-day,

CCLXXIX.

Had not some old ancestral clammer,
Once on a time obtained a " manor,"
    In which to cut his hay,
And somehow left it to come down
In safe succession to the one
    That occupies to-day!

CCLXXX.

These, for armorial bearings, had
Each three clams *clamant* and one shad,
    On their escutcheons graven;
And boasted of ancestral worth,
As far back as the fortieth birth
    That took place in West Haven.

CCLXXXI.

To prove this true, they first resort
To ancient records that are brought
    Down in ancestral tree,
And then to graveyards gravely go,
To hunt inscriptions, and to throw
    Light on their pedigree!

CCLXXXII.

This being done, 'tis found that they
Were born at least a century
    Before their stated time;
This reconciles anachronism,
And fills the gap in times abysm,
    Or their ancestral line!

CCLXXXIII.

Some others laid their claim to be
Ranked with the great "stuck-up-racy,"
    Upon their lack of brains;
Or rather insufficient skull,
To hold the little thimble-full,
    That each of theirs contains.

CCLXXXIV.

They had some money, it is true,
But then 'twas never earned, but grew
    Like pumpkin on a vine,
And dropped into their laps when ripe,
As I have seen a stricken snipe
    Drop from a shot of mine,

CCLXXXV.

Not into my own bag, but where
Some "lubber" bagged it in despair
    Of ever fetching feather ;
Just so their fortunes came to these
Land-lubbers, or " stuck-up-racies,"
    By chance shot of another !

CCLXXXVI.

And yet they toss their heads in air
As if all gravitation were
    Entirely suspended,
And tread the earth as if their feet
'Twixt heaven and earth might somewhere meet,
    If properly suspended !

CCLXXXVII.

Or grimly greet you in the street,
As if their vivisections met
    In spite of tied cravat,
And venture forth into the wind
With coat-tail streaming far behind,
    Like tail behind a rat!

CCLXXXVIII.

Now all of these pretentious airs,
Put on like sunday clothes of theirs,
    To cover up their vices,
Is what disgusts the Muse to see,
Provokes her taunts and raillery,
    And sting of cockatrices!

CCLXXXIX.

And though they ludicrously seem,
In gait and air, in port and mien,
    They scarcely merit laughter;
But only such a pitying glance
As folly catches in the dance,
    With vices dangling after!

CCXC.

But what disgusts the Muse still more,
Are vices rankling in the core
    Of all society;
Vices indigenously grown,
In church and state, and handed down
    As virtue's legacy!

CCXCI.

These vices bear their heads so high
In all church aristocracy,
    That virtue, meaner clad,
Mistakes her calling, and goes forth
In search of really honest worth,
    To pity and upbraid.

CCXCII.

There's Dea. Cantwell, whom you've seen
A hundred times upon the green,
    With sunday face so long,
That one would almost swear his nose
Ran half-way down to where his toes
    Notoriously belong!

CCXCIII.

He's been a deacon twenty years,
And yet, 'tis said, has sundry fears
    Of being damned at last;
But then such fears, his parson says,
Give evidence of special grace,
    And so he stands confessed!

CCXCIV.

But all his piety and grace
Are lavished on an ugly face,
    That all the uglier grows,
For putting on his solemn, grum
Demeanor, that is all a hum.,
    As every body knows!

CCXCV.

But then he's got the "solid rocks"
Converted once from fancy stocks,
   By sharper on the street;
And holds them in such durance vile
That they draw interest all the while,
   And yet no interest meet.

CCXCVI.

The bank has got them on deposit,
So "slyly" that nobody knows it;
   Yet rumor has it thus:—
It has them on what's called a "special,"
Not thereby meaning by the bushel,
   But for a special use.

CCXCVII.

It holds them "as" and "of" the deacon,
Two particles the lawyers stick on
   To entracts nice and witty;
Which means that when the bank "goes up,"
The deacon don't, but stays to sup
   With cashier in the city.

CCXCVIII.

Now should this bubble go unpunctured,
A little longer, Peter-Funkward,
   The deacon stands a chance,
Without a single risk, to "double,"
As brokers call it, when they gobble
   A fortune in advance.

CCXCIX.

Now all the while the deacon knows
The Bank's not worth the debts it owes,
 And may "go up" to-morrow,
And yet he lets its paper slide
From out his wallet gaping wide
 For bonds of those that borrow,

CCC.

And *this* is christian honesty!
Commands a premium to-day
 In the West Haven market!
Obtains your deaconships and makes,
Respectable your very rakes,
 However much they "lark it."

CCCI.

While honest poverty is spurned
The very door, and e'en out-turned
 The church, because it dares
To wear an independent front,
To have its say—its will, its wont,
 In church and state affairs!

CCCII.

And shall the Muse withhold her lash
From "potent, grave and reverend" cash,
 Or rather reverend *shin*.
With *plastering* suffix, just to hide,
Its naked leprosy outside,
 And villainy within?

CCCIII.

Not if all Wall-Street raised its head,
And swore that heaven and earth were made,
    To steadily revolve
On paper axis, held at par,
When gold is up to eighty-four,
    With tendencies above!

CCCIV.

And this your wretched paper bubble
Is all a sham, a cheat, a bauble,
    A sheer inflated lie;
The only bottom it has got
Is what it has, and yet has not,—
    A kite with string to fly!

CCCV.

And yet it has the potent power
To grind to earth the laboring poor,
    And make them doubly slave;
Enhancing value where 'tis not,
With "here you see it—there you don't,"
    Like thimble rigging knave!

CCCVI.

Of all the vices of the town—
And damning vices it has some,—
    There's none with this compares:—
The vice that steals from out your purse,
With knavish hand, to reimburse
    With *what the beggar wears!*

CCCVII.

One of its victims I had known,
A youth once worshiped through the town
    For every manly grace;
Though neither rich, nor yet high-bred,
He wore an honest front, and had
    As true a heart as face.

CCCVIII.

He married young ('twas no disgrace
To marry thus in earlier days,)
    And had as sweet a wife
As ever heaven smiled down upon,—
And one as beautiful as young,
    And full of joyous life.

CCCIX.

They lived a brief way out of town;
Their little cottage painted brown,
    Was tasteful in design,
And had a neat veranda, where
Each climbing rose perfumed the air,
    As well as clambering vine!

CCCX.

He was employed by Cant & Co.,
Upon a salary too low,
    They thought, for him to live;
So they discharged him, lest his wife
Should tempt to more expensive life,
    Or to purloin and thieve!

CCCXI

And yet this pious firm proposes
To aid their clerk, if he but chooses,
    By making him a loan;
He giving bond and mortgage back,
Upon his house, and little tract
    Of land, just out of town.

CCCXII.

The loan that they would have him take,
Is in the bills that they protect,
    On the Gridiron Bank;
An institution they extol
As having all its capital
    In stocks of highest rank!

CCCXIII.

Its paper they would have him hold
Against such time as they the gold
    May purchase up at par,
When they, of course, will promptly make
Redemption of the bills in bank,
    Or pay in trade before!

CCCXIV.

And thus the tempters of this youth,
The one a deacon now forsooth,
    Adroitly fling their twine;
As satan once for Eve laid wait,
And knew that nibbling at the bait,
    Was dangling at the line!

CCCXV.

The young man sees the gilded fly,
And though at first a little shy,
    Takes greedy hold at last;
The deacon slowly winds his reel,
He knows he's hooked with hook of steel,
    And to his twine made fast!

CCCXVI.

A brief month passes, and what then?
A mad, tumultuous rush of men,
    All clamorous through the street;
The great unpunctured bubble's burst,
" Gone up," is " nowhere," or a-dust
    Amidst their trampling feet!

CCCXVII.

The young man's hopes, all stowed away
'Neath trusty lock and trustier key,
    Come forth to light at last;
One stifled curse, one bitter groan,
And all his dreams of wealth are flown,
    Like shadows madly grasped,

CCCXVIII.

At first he struggles manfully,
Like some strong swimmer on the sea,
    Whose bark has just gone down
'Neath crushing iceberg, leaving there
Nor sign of life nor splint of spar,
    To rest a hope upon!

CCCXIX.

But soon the waters o'er his soul
In wild tumultuous horror roll,
    While reason from her throne
Reels headlong, and you hear a cry
Of deepest mortal agony
    Above the waters borne!

CCCXX.

Go to that little cottage now:—
Just heaven! ward off the impending blow
    From that devoted head,
Now pillowed on the feverish breast
Of him who tosts in wild unrest,
    And mutters words scarce heard!

CCCXXI.

To morrow sees that bond mature:—
The dying man has struggled o'er
    The brink of his despair,
Yet raves all wildly; strong men stay
To hold him in his agony,
    And wish they were not there!

CCCXXII.

The deacon calls to get his pay:—
He had not heard the news that day,
    Or he had staid at home;
The dying man he does not see,
But hears one cry of agony,
    And rushes from the room!

CCCXXIII.

The evening sun goes down at last:—
All earthly joy and grief are past,
    To that strong sufferer now;
His bond of life lies cancelled there,
You see the pall, the hearse, the bier,
    The widow's weeds of woe!

CCCXXIV.

But there's another bond to meet:—
Death summons all with equal feet,
    The monarch as the slave,
But has no power to cancel those
Most potent bonds the lawyers use
    To reach beyond the grave!

CCCXXV.

The deacon calls a few weeks later:—
He is, in fact, no woman hater,
    So seeks the widow's door,
In hopes she's found some special grace
To lighten up her dark distress,
    Since his day's grace is o'er!

CCCXXVI.

He's called to see what she can do:—
The widow hears his story through;
    The mortgage covers all,—
All to the very plate he brought,
In all his wealth of love unbought,
    To contract marital!

CCCXXVII.

His pay is finally obtained :—
Foreclosure, bills of cost, suit gained—
   A writ of restitution;
All hurried through in "double quick,"
And in the sheriff's hands to prick
   The bubble—destitution!

CCCXXVIII.

Ah Dea. Cant, the day will come,
When heaven on all such deeds shall frown,
   And you will plead in vain,
As Dives did with Lazarus,
For one small drop to quench your thirst,
   Or stay your fiery pain!

CCCXXIX.

The great eternal, primal law
Of compensation, has no flaw,
   Or subterfuge for you;
It doles you out for every sin
A curse for you to swelter in,
   When Hades has its due!

CCCXXX.

Oh, how I do detest their cant,
These long-eared puritans that rant
   About old Adam's sin,
Who, some two thousand years before
The flood, (the Brahmins make it more,)
   Got strangely taken in!

CCCXXXI.

And who, because their sins are great,
Lay all the blame on Adam's pate,
    Or rather on his loins;
Or fancy, when themselves miscarry,
'Tis not themselves, but some young Harry,
    Fresh from the *Old* ones groins!

CCCXXXII.

To whip the devil round the stump
Is mean enough, but when you thump
    Him squarely o'er the pate,
With your own sins, 'tis dastardly,
And though I hate the devil, I
    Will help him in such strait!

CCCXXXIII.

He's had his sins to answer for,
As Milton shows; and when the power
    That hurled him headlong down
The outer battlements, and sent
His hosts sky-voyaging, had once spent
    Its force,— he was "done brown!"

CCCXXXIV.

This is no theologic marvel,
But settled fact beyond all cavil,
    Except 'mong pagan powers;
And hence, I've always felt the church
Had its foundation built too much
    On Adam's sin, not ours!

CCCXXXV.

Had we all sinned in Adam's fall,
Then Adam must have sinned for all,
    Or done up all our sinning,
At least six thousand years before
We ever thought of sinning, or
    Had our tadpole begining!

CCCXXXVI.

Now this would utterly reverse
That great hereditary curse
    From sire to son inbred,
And send the sins of which we boast,
Like chickens, vilely back to roost
    On Adam's guiltless head!

CCCXXXVII.

And though I solemnly protest,
As well for Adam as the rest
    Of our ancestral line,
Against such vile injustice done
To primal sire, when looked upon
    As guilty of our crime;

CCCXXXVIII.

Yet I admit we bear his sin,
And feel the curse pronounced on him,
    As the Church Creed declares;
But not as those believe who say,
All sin through him, and thus bewray
    His sins alone, not *theirs*.

CCCXXXIX.

A better faith from me receive,
And act upon it while you live,
   And longer if you can:—
Believe that every thought and word,
And deed of yours, stands registered

CCCXL.

   Against you to a man,
And that on reaching that High Court
Of Chancery, where all resort
   For ultimate decree,
That each must answer for his own,
From Adam down to his last son,
   In chain of pedigree;

CCCXLI.

That none can plead another's sin
In bar of judgment against him,
   In that Imperial Court,
Where justice sits with equal scales
And in her judgments never fails
   To weigh the secret thought,

CCCXLII.

As well as overt act of crime;
Accept this faith as yours and mine,
   And then we may deceive
The devil, with his imps and elves,
But never can deceive ourselves,
   The longest day we live!

CCCXLIII.

Their work is ended.   He whose life
In christian grace was all too brief,
   Has gone to rest at last;—
With him all earthly toils are o'er,
All griefs and joys forevermore,
   With life's brief journey, past.

CCCXLIV.

He sleeps all tranquilly, this good,
Devout, and lowly man of God,—
   Rests from his toils in peace;
And they who smote him in the dust,
With cruel wrong and acts accurst,
   Have of their hate surcease.

CCCXLV.

Life's journey ended—he sleeps well;
No feuds to meet, no broils to quell,
   No clamors to allay;
No call to dry the widow's tear,
No mourner's grief to seek and share,
   No broken hearts to stay.

CCCXLVI.

With him the storms of life are spent,
No cloud remains its wrath to vent,
   All is serene and clear;—
And He who spans the heavens above
With rain-bow tokens of his love,
   Accords a welcome there!

CCCXLVII.

Hate, like a scorpion, ever dies
From its own sting.   Its agonies
   Are those itself out-throes;
Then let the venom of the few,
Who on his church such scandal drew,
   Die as the scorpion does!

www.ingramcontent.com/pod-product-compliance
Lightning Source LLC
Chambersburg PA
CBHW020301090426
42735CB00009B/1174